ANOTHER

QUILT DESIGNS
COLORING BOOK
FOR ADULTS

78 Named Quilt Blocks
plus
38 Traditional Patchwork Quilt
Coloring Pages
to
Color and Embellish

the Green-Eyed-Lady
Books.SmartSeniorpreneur.com

Thank You for Your Purchase!

I want you to have the best possible experience using this coloring book. Even though the coloring designs are printed on only one side of the page, I strongly recommend using coloring pencils. There's a good possibility that some gel pens, markers and ink liners may bleed through the paper and mar the pages beneath.

For this reason, **I suggest that you either place a piece of heavy paper or card stock or even a cereal box back behind the page you're working on, or carefully cut the page out using a razor-type craft knife and color directly on your work surface.** In fact, you might want to cut out the pages or use light cardboard between pages if you tend to be heavy-handed with your pencils. This way, there won't be impressions left behind on the other pages.

I have included a "tester page" of quilt patch designs where you can test your pens and pencils for bleeding, and try out color blending and layering techniques. Find it on page 2. Again, if you are trying out markers, put a shield of some kind behind that page as you test.

New with this version is an **alphabetical visual index** to each of the 78 quilt blocks used. They're shaded to give you an idea of how you might want to color but those shadings are simply suggestions - feel free to do your own thing!

Enjoy the relaxing effects of coloring in this book, and please share your experience with others by leaving a review.

Happy Coloring!

the Green-Eyed Lady

1

Test Page

Star of Bethlehem

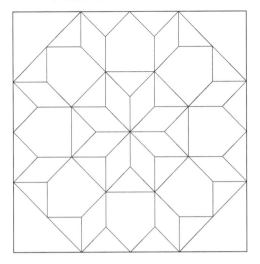

Crown of Thorns

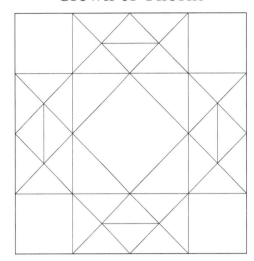

Pineapple

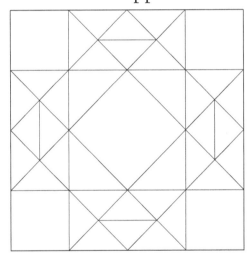

Fireworks

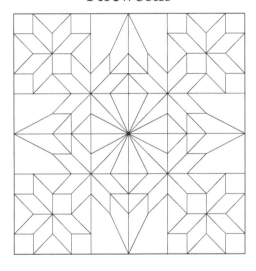

Double Windmill

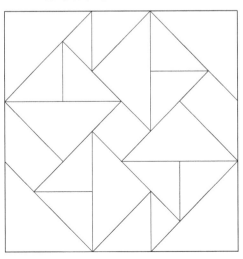

Lady of the Lake

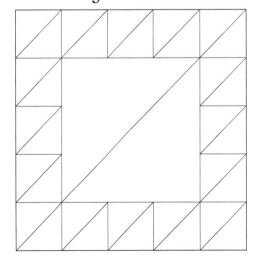

Star of Bethlehem & Crown of Thorns

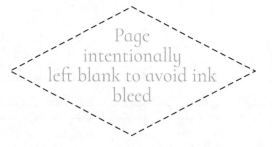

Page intentionally left blank to avoid ink bleed

Pineapple

Page intentionally left blank to avoid ink bleed

Page
intentionally
left blank to avoid ink
bleed

Wyoming Valley

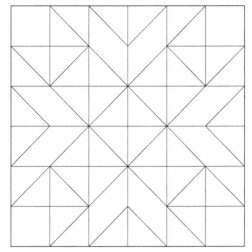

Apple Pie

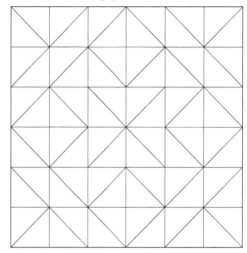

Lucky Clover

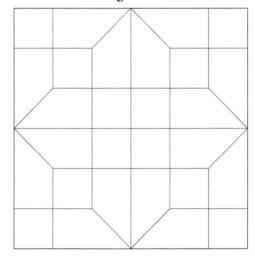

Five Spot

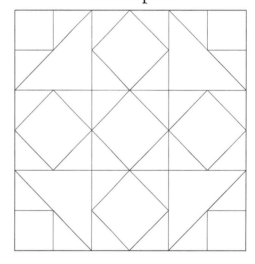

Aunt Dinah

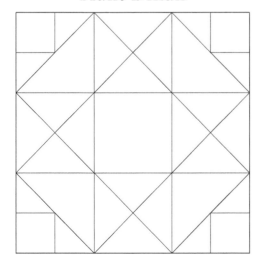

Album Quilt

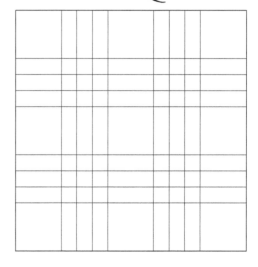

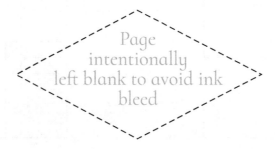
Page
intentionally
left blank to avoid ink
bleed

Wyoming Valley & Apple Pie

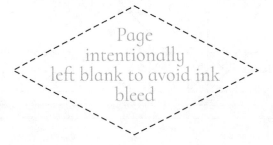
Page
intentionally
left blank to avoid ink
bleed

Lucky Clovers

Page
intentionally
left blank to avoid ink
bleed

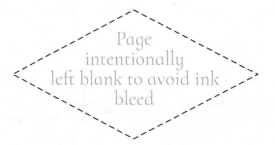
Page
intentionally
left blank to avoid ink
bleed

Monkey Wrench

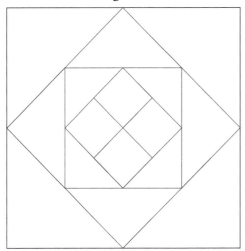

Martha Washington's Star

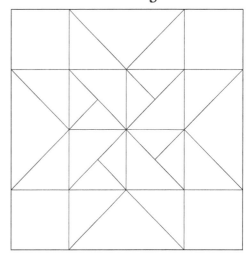

Magic Circle

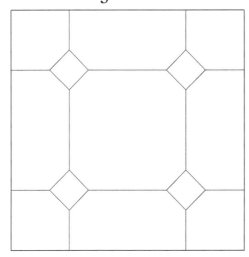

Fox Chase

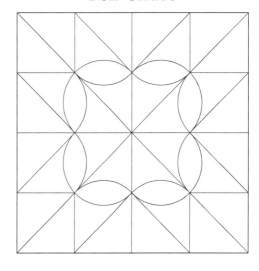

Stars & Pinwheels

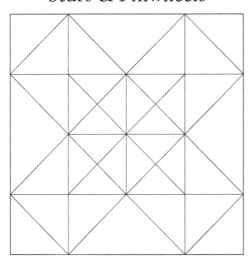

Carpenter's Wheel

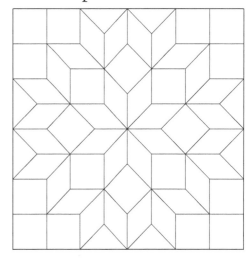

Page
intentionally
left blank to avoid ink
bleed

Monkey Wrench

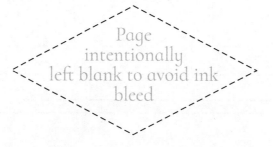
Page intentionally left blank to avoid ink bleed

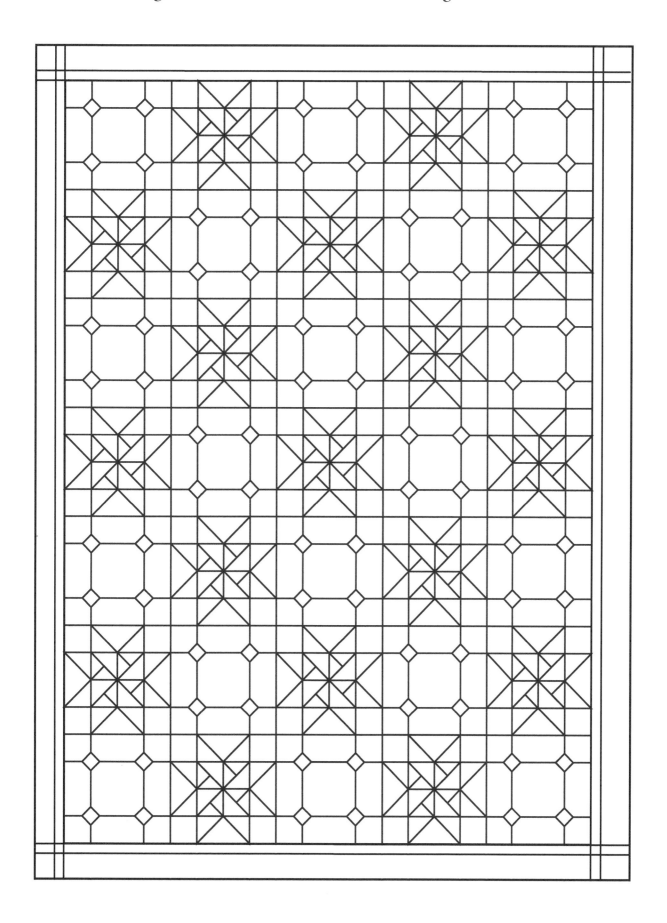

Page
intentionally
left blank to avoid ink
bleed

Fox Chase & Stars and Pinwheels

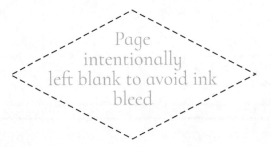
Page
intentionally
left blank to avoid ink
bleed

All Hallows

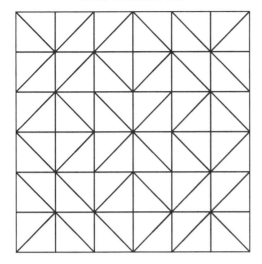

Summer Winds

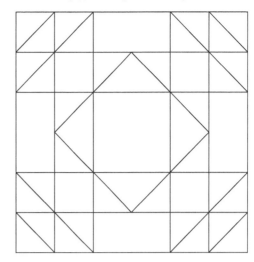

Hither & Yon

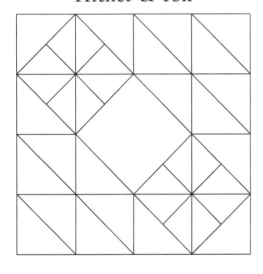

Yankee Puzzle

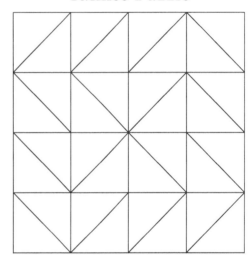

Four by Two

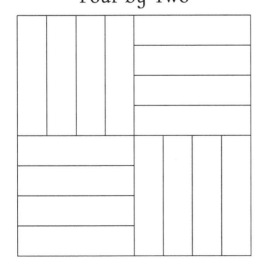

Double X No. 3

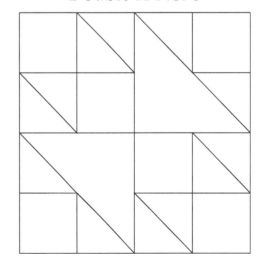

Page
intentionally
left blank to avoid ink
bleed

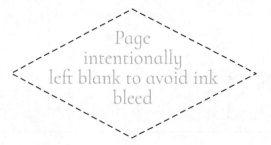
Page
intentionally
left blank to avoid ink
bleed

Page intentionally left blank to avoid ink bleed

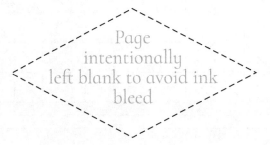

Page intentionally left blank to avoid ink bleed

34

Card Basket

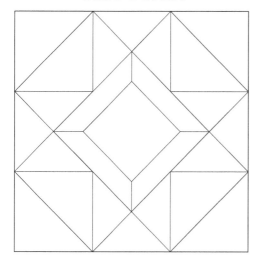

Little Rock Block

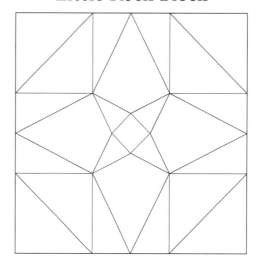

London Roads

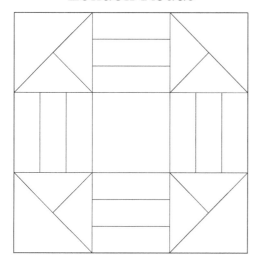

Sunbeam

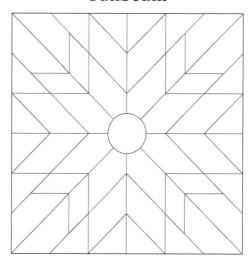

Optical Illusion

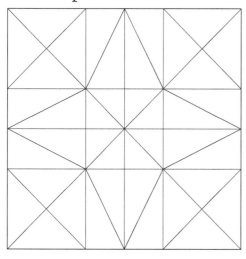

Duck and Ducklings

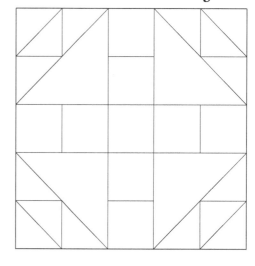

Card Basket & Little Rock Block

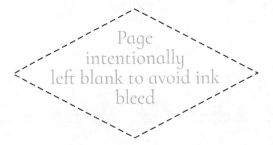
Page
intentionally
left blank to avoid ink
bleed

London Roads & Sunbeam

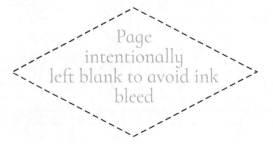
Page
intentionally
left blank to avoid ink
bleed

Optical Illusion

Page intentionally left blank to avoid ink bleed

Grandma's Favorite

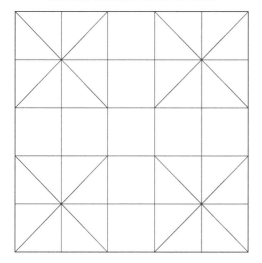

Odd Scraps Patchwork

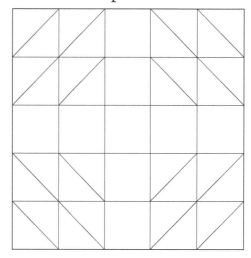

Whirling Star

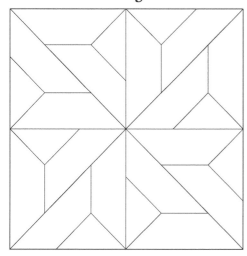

Clown's Choice

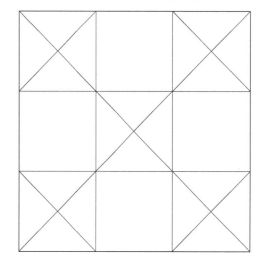

Practical Orchard

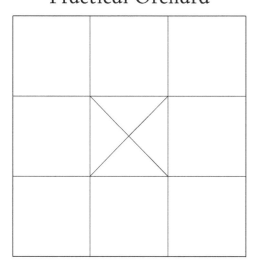

Lena's Choice

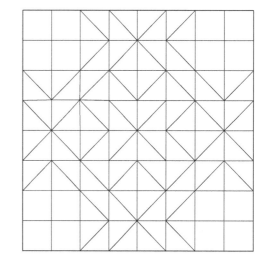

44

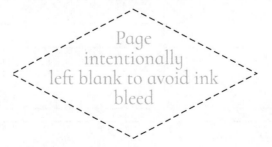

Page
intentionally
left blank to avoid ink
bleed

Whirling Stars

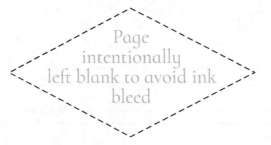

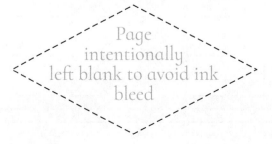
Page intentionally left blank to avoid ink bleed

Meadow Flower

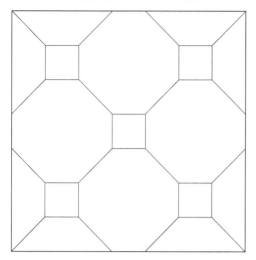

Oatmeal Raisin Cookie

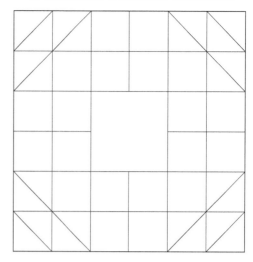

Silver Maple

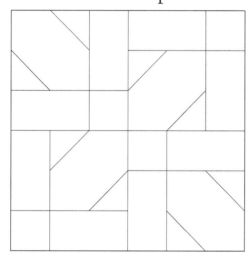

Bird of Paradise

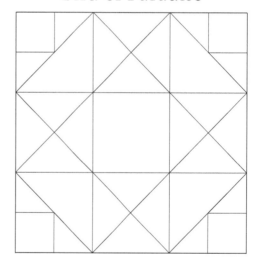

Fox and Geese

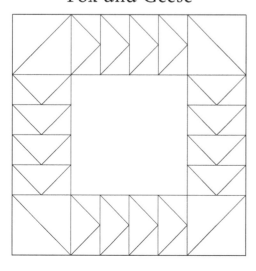

Linton

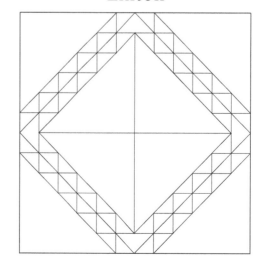

Page
intentionally
left blank to avoid ink
bleed

Meadow Flowers

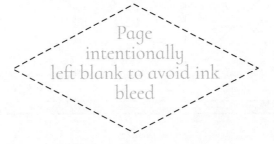
Page
intentionally
left blank to avoid ink
bleed

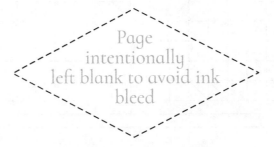

Page
intentionally
left blank to avoid ink
bleed

Page
intentionally
left blank to avoid ink
bleed

Game Cocks

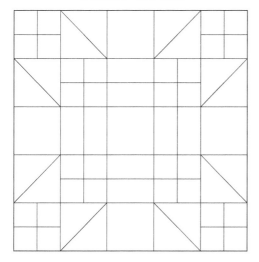

Offset Squares

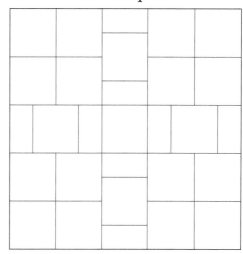

Joseph's Coat

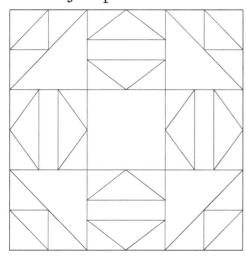

Turnstile

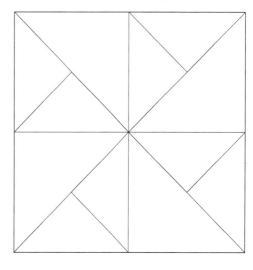

Blockade

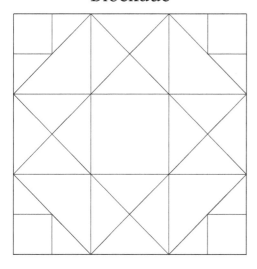

Fool's Square

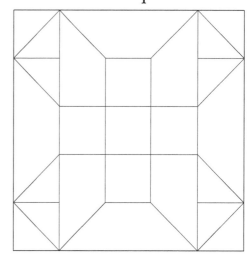

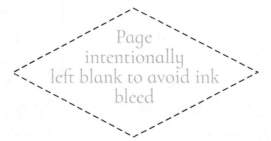
Page intentionally left blank to avoid ink bleed

Game Cocks & Offset Squares

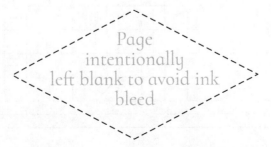
Page
intentionally
left blank to avoid ink
bleed

Joseph's Coat

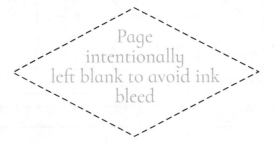
Page intentionally left blank to avoid ink bleed

Turnstile & Blockade

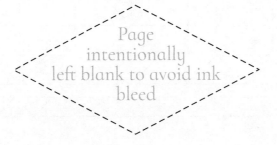
Page intentionally left blank to avoid ink bleed

Blue Boutonneires

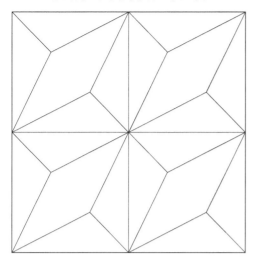

Girl's Favorite

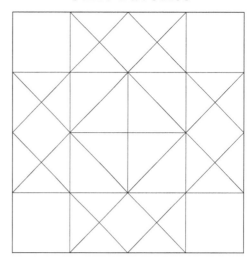

School Girl's Puzzle

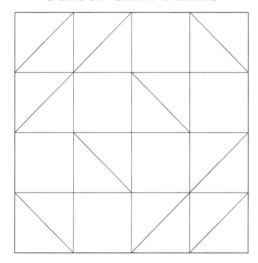

Providence Block

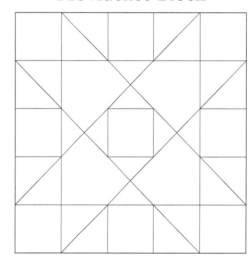

Illusion

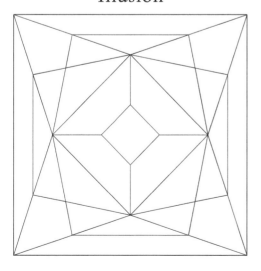

Flying X

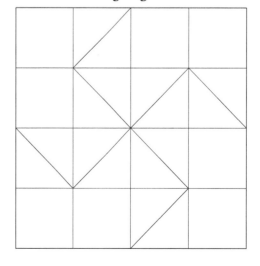

Blue Boutonneires

Page
intentionally
left blank to avoid ink
bleed

Page
intentionally
left blank to avoid ink
bleed

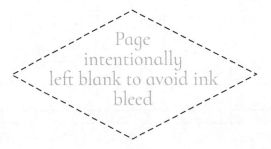
Page
intentionally
left blank to avoid ink
bleed

Nine Patch Star

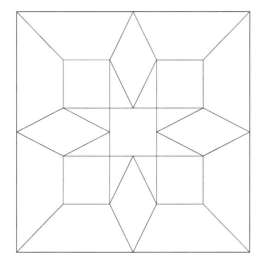

Patch as Patch Can

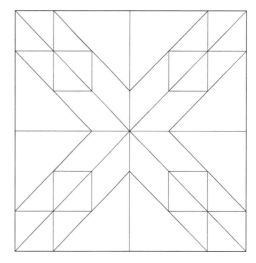

LeMoyne Star

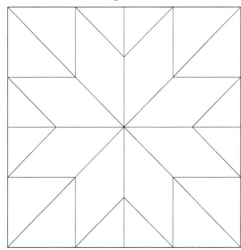

Star of North Carolina

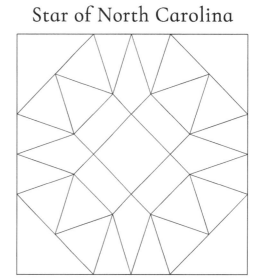

Calico Puzzle

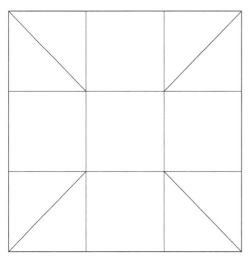

Four Times Nine

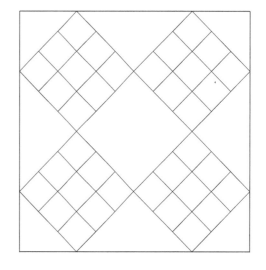

Page
intentionally
left blank to avoid ink
bleed

Nine-Patch Star & Patch as Patch Can

Page
intentionally
left blank to avoid ink
bleed

LeMoyne Star

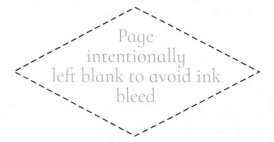

Page
intentionally
left blank to avoid ink
bleed

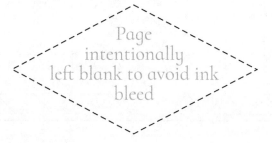
Page
intentionally
left blank to avoid ink
bleed

Four-X Star

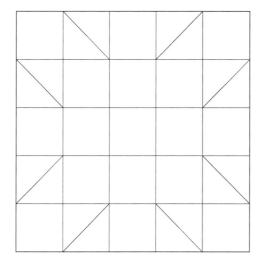

Country Crown

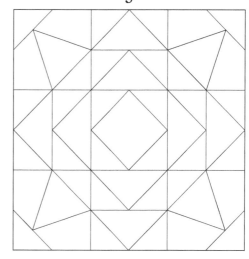

Blueberry Pie

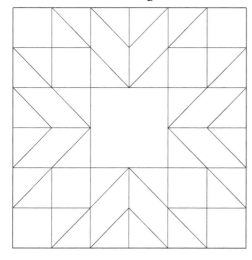

Full-Blown Tulip

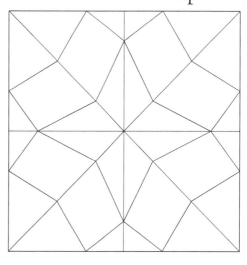

Mollie's Choice

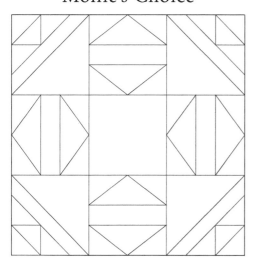

Old Maid's Ramble

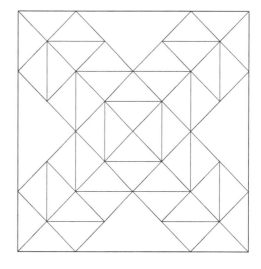

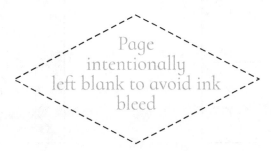
Page
intentionally
left blank to avoid ink
bleed

Country Crown & Blueberry Pie

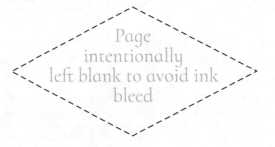
Page
intentionally
left blank to avoid ink
bleed

Full-Blown Tulip & Mollie's Choice

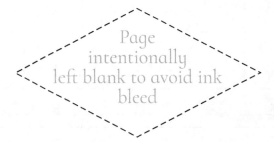
Page
intentionally
left blank to avoid ink
bleed

Page
intentionally
left blank to avoid ink
bleed

Devil's Puzzle

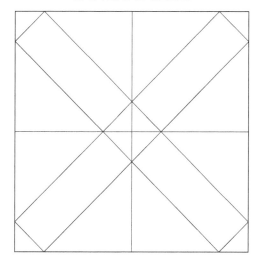

New Star

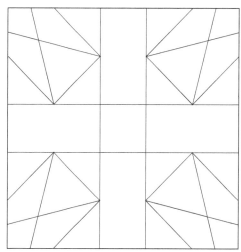

Garden of Eden

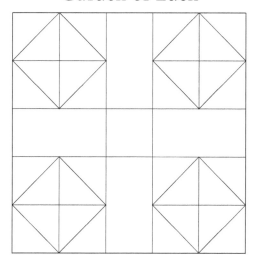

Cross Within Cross

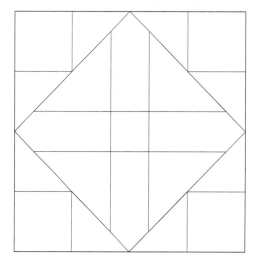

Dad's Bow Tie

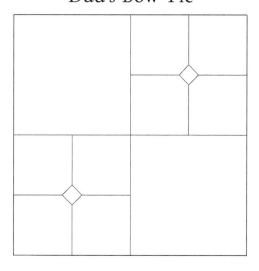

King's Crown

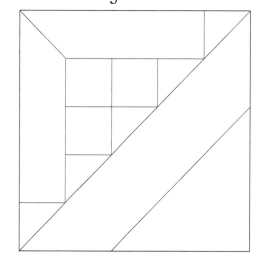

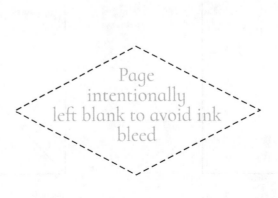
Page
intentionally
left blank to avoid ink
bleed

Page
intentionally
left blank to avoid ink
bleed

Cross Within Cross & Dad's Bow Tie

Page
intentionally
left blank to avoid ink
bleed

King's Crown

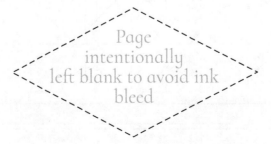

Page
intentionally
left blank to avoid ink
bleed

Jig Jog Puzzle

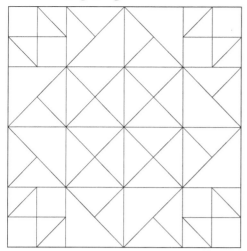

Carrie Nation Block

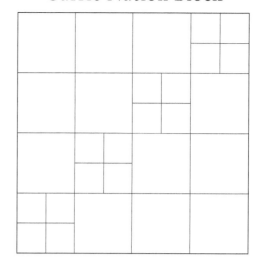

Lost Children

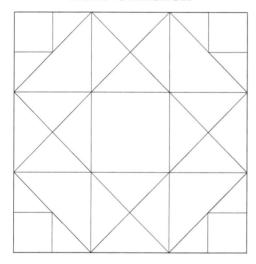

Star Puzzle

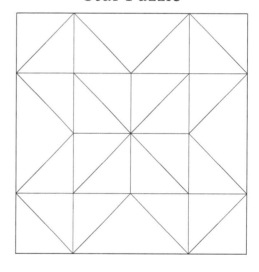

Goose Tracks

Eight Hands Around

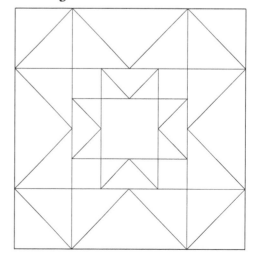

Page
intentionally
left blank to avoid ink
bleed

Vortex

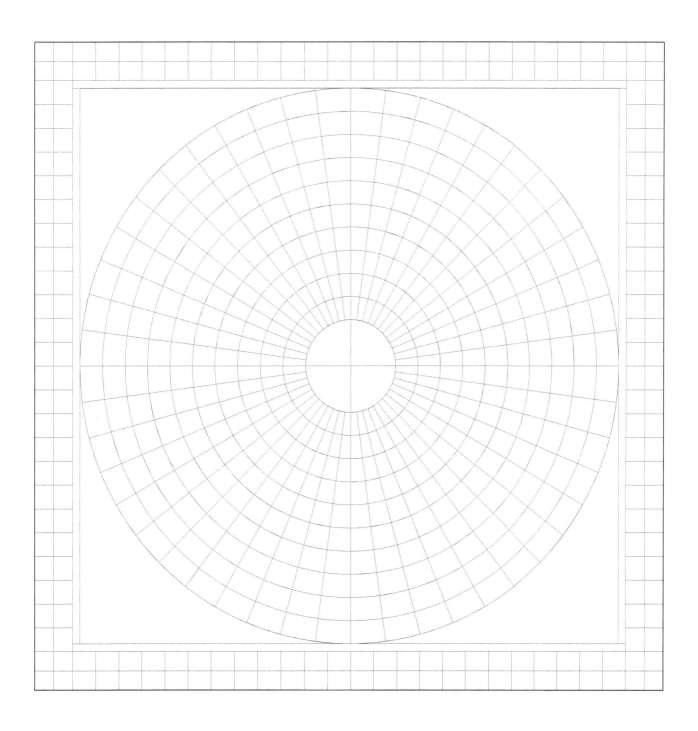

Page intentionally left blank to avoid ink bleed

Lone Star

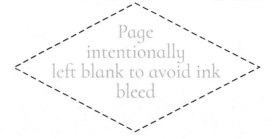
Page
intentionally
left blank to avoid ink
bleed

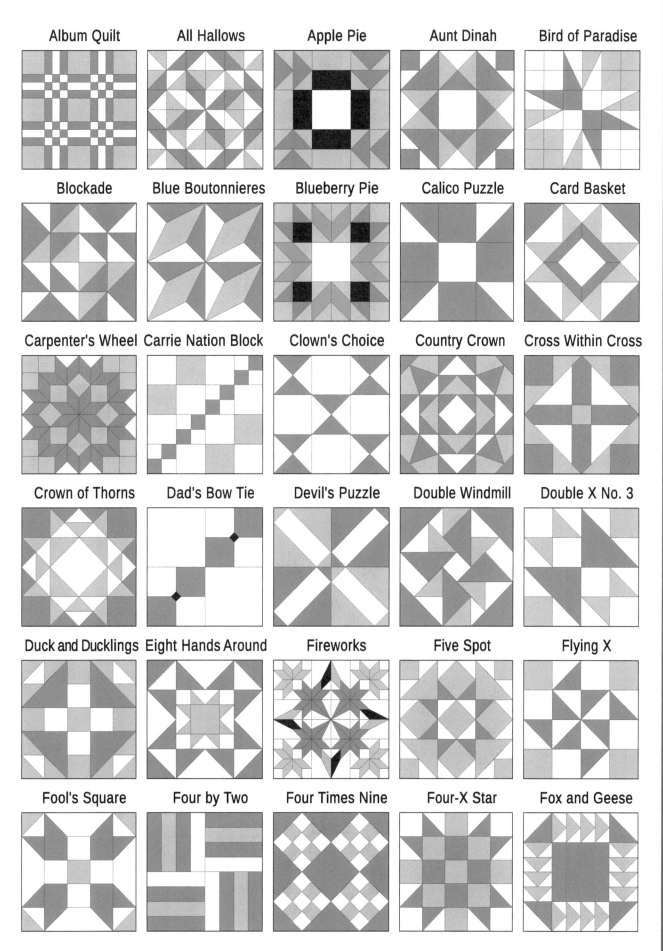

Album Quilt	All Hallows	Apple Pie	Aunt Dinah	Bird of Paradise
Blockade	Blue Boutonnieres	Blueberry Pie	Calico Puzzle	Card Basket
Carpenter's Wheel	Carrie Nation Block	Clown's Choice	Country Crown	Cross Within Cross
Crown of Thorns	Dad's Bow Tie	Devil's Puzzle	Double Windmill	Double X No. 3
Duck and Ducklings	Eight Hands Around	Fireworks	Five Spot	Flying X
Fool's Square	Four by Two	Four Times Nine	Four-X Star	Fox and Geese

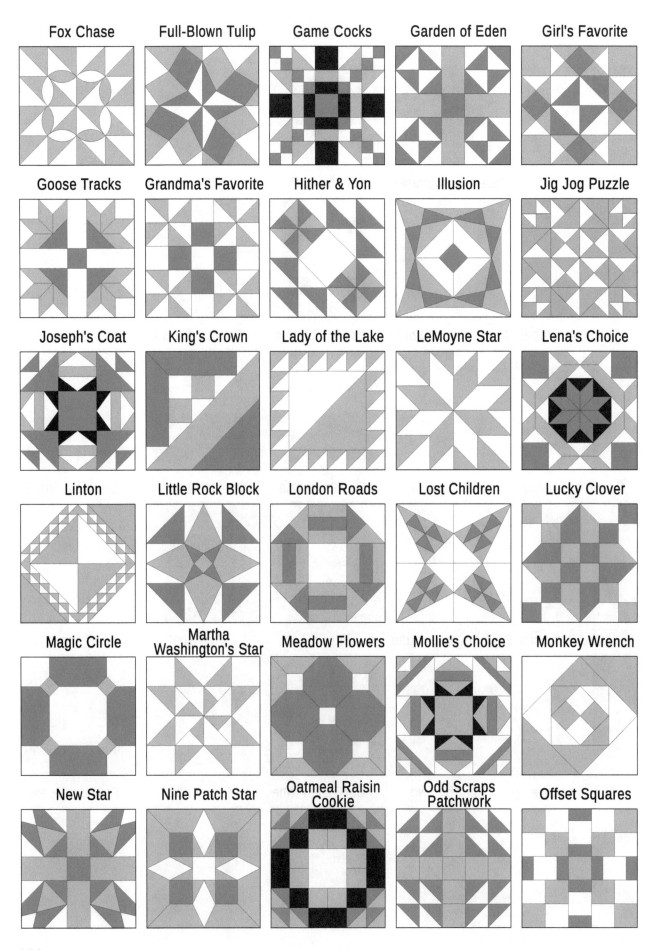

Fox Chase	Full-Blown Tulip	Game Cocks	Garden of Eden	Girl's Favorite
Goose Tracks	Grandma's Favorite	Hither & Yon	Illusion	Jig Jog Puzzle
Joseph's Coat	King's Crown	Lady of the Lake	LeMoyne Star	Lena's Choice
Linton	Little Rock Block	London Roads	Lost Children	Lucky Clover
Magic Circle	Martha Washington's Star	Meadow Flowers	Mollie's Choice	Monkey Wrench
New Star	Nine Patch Star	Oatmeal Raisin Cookie	Odd Scraps Patchwork	Offset Squares

Old Maid's Ramble   Optical Illusion   Patch as Patch Can   Pineapple   Practical Orchard

Providence Block   School Girl's Puzzle   Silver Maple   Star of Bethlehem   Star of North Carolina

Star Puzzle   Stars & Pinwheels   Summer Winds   Sunbeam   Turnstile

Whirling Star   Wyoming Valley   Yankee Puzzle

Vortex Quilt   Lone Star Quilt

Also Available from Green-Eyed Lady

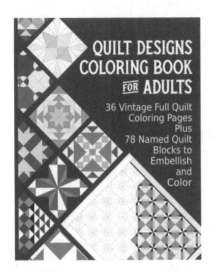

Book #1 in my *Stress-Reliever Coloring Books for Grown-ups* Series, this book includes a few vintage applique quilts to color in addition to plenty of patchwork.

Follow this link to purchase on Amazon:
https://www.bklnk.com/B08JDTRJ3B

or scan the code below with your phone's camera

Scan Me

Want to help others?

A favor, please...

 Hi, I'm the Green-Eyed Lady and creator of this coloring book.

If you enjoyed it, I'd really appreciate your taking 30 seconds to leave an **HONEST REVIEW** so others can benefit from your insights.

I don't have a big publishing house behind me that can spend thousands of dollars on marketing -- it's just me - a one-person home-based publishing business. So I depend very heavily on honest reviews from good people like you to help "get the word out" when my books are good (and/or give feedback on how I can improve them when they're not so good).

Believe it or not, I read all reviews personally. I really do care about what you have to say.

Thank you in advance!

To leave a review, just go to

www.amazon.com/review/create-review?&asin=B08WJTPVBW

or scan the image below with your phone camera.

Scan Me to Leave a Review...

Made in United States
Troutdale, OR
12/02/2024

25654759R00064